IN TIMES OF DISASTER

Jennifer Tuckett,
Dorothy Fortenberry
&
Lauren Feldman

BROADWAY PLAY PUBLISHING INC
New York
www.broadwayplaypublishing.com
info@broadwayplaypublishing.com

IN TIMES OF DISASTER
  © Copyright 2006:
WAYS YOU CAN SURVIVE THE WORLD
  by Jennifer Tuckett
AFTER THE FLOOD by Dorothy Fortenberry
WHEN IT RAINS by Lauren Feldman

Cover photo by Jacques-Jean Tiziou

First printing: March 2006
This printing: October 2017
I S B N: 978-0-88145-310-2

Book design: Marie Donovan
Word processing: Microsoft Word
Typographic controls: Ventura Publisher
Typeface: Palatino

CONTENTS

PREFACE

Yale School of Drama is proud to produce the work of
some of the nation's most gifted young playwrights.
The School is unique among professional training
programs in welcoming talented students with
leadership potential in every discipline of the theater;
in emphasizing breadth of opportunities to collaborate
in production; and in embracing artists in training
within the professional environment of Yale Repertory
Theatre. And when it comes to playwriting, the School
of Drama makes an unparalleled commitment to the
production of new plays—the most important theater
experience for which we can prepare artists in the 21st
century.

This collection of plays represents the highest
aspirations of the Yale School of Drama. As good
as they are, they honor the legacy of great American
dramatists who have studied here in New Haven.
They are also symbols of our national investment
in the range of our students' imaginations. They are
harbingers of ideas to come—from just three of the
young artists who are the bright future of the nation's,
and the world's, theater.

James Bundy, Dean, Yale School of Drama

INTRODUCTION

IN TIMES OF DISASTER introduces three exciting new playwrights, all first-year students in the Playwriting Department of the Yale School of Drama, all born within six months of each other; one from Miami, one from DC, one from England. Seven months ago, I became chairman of this department, and Lauren Feldman, Dorothy Fortenberry and Jennifer Tuckett are the first class that I have selected myself.

Last September at the beginning of classes, we first met together, in a hot basement rehearsal room (our classroom), to discuss what they were going to write. They decided on a series of short plays that would somehow relate to one another, that would have something (they didn't know what) in common, and which would perhaps illuminate each other. These young women are very engaged in the world, both politically and socially, so it was no surprise that last September the tragedy of Hurricane Katrina was on all of their minds. New Orleans, they soon agreed, would become the first link or theme. From there, the themes broadened out, but they never lost sight that though they were writing their own plays, in their own very distinct styles, their plays would somehow connect, even comment upon, the others. We met for three hours a week; spent an hour on each of their plays. They watched each other's weekly progress; encouraged and supported one another. To write together with other writers—this is something I have rarely been allowed to experience myself. In watching these three talented women create a unified beautiful evening of theater, without losing their own distinct voices, or compromising their interests, made me both envious and proud.

As you will see, IN TIMES OF DISASTER has a great deal of direct address; this is of course on purpose. Lauren, Dorothy and Jenny have a lot to say about some very important things, and, I think, they wish to say much of this directly to us. They have stories to tell us, characters who want to share with us, they have hopes, fears, anxieties. And they are angry about what their world has become. A deep and clear moral center runs through these plays, all of which ask us to look not only at our lives but at the state of our world. Only twenty-six years old, these three playwrights can still remember what it was like to believe in things and be innocent, so it is even all the more heartbreaking when they show us how far from innocence our world has come.

Richard Nelson, New Haven CT, March 2006

IN TIMES OF DISASTER was first performed on
16 March 2006 at Yale School of Drama, New Haven,
Connecticut (James Bundy, Dean) with the following
cast and creative contributors:

WAYS YOU CAN SURVIVE THE WORLD

YASMIN/MARY .... Sofia Gomez
MIRANDA/KATIE/AZMA .... Brooke Parks

Director .... Michael Donahue
Stage Manager .... Ryan Durham
Associate Festival Producer .... Jason Fitzgerald

AFTER THE FLOOD

ANNETTE/SISTER CLARICE/SUZANNE ..Lisa Birnbaum
LUCILLE/MICHELLE .... Erin Buckley
ALTHEA ....Sarita Covington
TOM/PATRICK/HERBERT .... Alex Major
ROSE/SARAH/TIBBY .... Amanda Warren

Director .... Shana Cooper
Stage Manager .... Lisa Shuster
Associate Festival Producer ....Drew Lichtenberg
Dialect Advisor .... Beth McGuire

WHEN IT RAINS

SOUP .... Aubyn Philabaum
LYNN .... Kathleen McElfresh

Director .... Snehal Desai
Stage Managers ...... Katrina Olson, Derek DiGregorio
Associate Festival Producer .... Joseph Cermatori

The Associate Production Supervisor for the entire
festival was Jonathan Reed. The Festival Director was
Rebecca Rugg.

WAYS YOU CAN SURVIVE THE WORLD
PART ONE: BE A SUPERHERO
Jennifer Tuckett

CHARACTERS & SETTING

YASMIN, *aged thirteen*
MIRANDA, YASMIN's *doctor.*

The characters in the three Parts should be played by two actresses. YASMIN and MARY should be played by the same actress. MIRANDA, KATIE and AZMA should be played by the same actress.

The set should be minimal and does not need to be realistic.

Scene One

(Lights rise on MIRANDA, *a doctor in her thirties, working at her desk. Lights fade.)*

(Lights rise on YASMIN.*)*

YASMIN: Sometimes you feel as if you just have to save the world. You do. You may be thirteen (like I am). You may be short and of an embarrassingly slight build (like I am). You may be forced to wear your hair in pigtails and to smother your eyes with thick rimmed glasses like the ones they prescribe for people on the N H S or without health insurance. But still. You can't shake off that nagging feeling that you'd really better save the world soon or else you'll never be able to get a proper night's sleep before school.
(She hesitates.)
Last night, I am watching the television in the living room as I wait for my mother to come home from work. It is about eight o'clock at night and I should be doing my homework but I can't and the reason I can't is because I can't take my eyes off the television screen and the reason I can't take my eyes off the television screen is because the images of war and death and terrorism and floods that are flashing before my eyes and which I have seen so many times before so that I almost don't notice them anymore have suddenly begun to get muddled up in my head until it seems as if all these things—the war, the terrorist attacks, the floods—are all happening in my living room at once and that the only thing to do is make for the Ark but, of course, no one has told me where it's leaving from

because even if there was such a thing I can't see God choosing a bespectacled, half-British, half-Pakistani thirteen year old as one of the two human beings out of everyone who he's going to choose to save. I'm just not that lucky.
(Beat)
And it is then that it happens. Just as I'm beginning to panic about the idea of there not being an ark, and that I'll be stuck in the living room, eyes glued to the television screen forever or at least until the water rises over us both, I suddenly feel myself gradually rising up from the ground. At first I am hovering only half an inch above the sofa or so and so I can tell myself that this is just a trick of my imagination but as soon as I do, I find myself rising rapidly until the top of my head is brushing the ceiling and I can no longer see the images on television anymore.
(Beat)
And it is then that I stop rising and I start falling and I hit the ground with a bump and for a moment I think I am going to go right through the springs of our old sofa, but I don't, which is a good thing, as flying or not, my mother would never forgive me for that.
(Pause)
For a long time. For a long time. For a long time. I. I. I sit in stunned silence on the sofa. And then...gradually...I realise the truth. I am a superhero. This is why I have always felt as I have. I am not human at all. And, with this realisation, I am able to pry my eyes away from the television screen and I get up and go to bed.

(YASMIN *gets up and goes to bed. Lights fade.*)

Scene Two

(Lights rise on MIRANDA *at her desk.* YASMIN *sits opposite her.)*

MIRANDA: When I was six years old and in my second year at elementary school my teacher asked our class one day what did we want to be when we grew up. Well, this was a hard question for a group of six year olds, still getting used to the regime of lessons and letters and numbers and nap time, to answer and for a moment we sat on our blankets perplexed, some of us (I won't say who) occasionally sucking our thumb. And, for some strange reason, I can still vividly remember this day. I remember Tommy saying he'd like to be a Daddy when he grew up and Jack saying he'd like to be a fireman and others policemen or nurses and other things of this nature. And I remember when it was my turn I was very scared. Because I wanted to say that I wanted to be Superman when I grew up and get changed in a telephone box and be friends with Lois Lane and do all these really wonderful things. But I couldn't. I just couldn't say the words. I don't know why. I was scared of being laughed at, I suppose. And so I sat there in silence as the teacher asked all the other children what did they want to be when they grew up and when she turned to me and said "Miranda, you've been very quiet, why don't you tell us what you'd like to be?" I just shook my head and pulled my blanket over my face and I began to cry. *(She hesitates.)* And that's how I became a doctor.

YASMIN: That's a stupid story.

MIRANDA: I see.

YASMIN: I came to you with a serious condition. I'm not six years old.

MIRANDA: I'm not saying—

YASMIN: *(Insistently)* You are—

MIRANDA: Look. Yasmin. I'm just trying to explain. When I was younger, I thought that if I jumped off the roof and waved my arms really fast I would take to flight.

YASMIN: But I wasn't—

MIRANDA: Or if I held onto lots and lots of helium balloons, I would be taken up into the air.

YASMIN: I wasn't—

MIRANDA: Or if I made a parachute from a sheet, I would soar among the clouds.

YASMIN: I wasn't—

MIRANDA: But, in my heart, I knew I wouldn't, Yasmin. And that's why I never jumped off the roof.

(She looks at YASMIN. YASMIN *hesitates.)*

YASMIN: *(Slowly)* But that was just... you giving up.

*(*MIRANDA *frowns.)*

YASMIN: Because there are such things as real superheroes.

*(*MIRANDA *hesitates.)*

YASMIN: *(Insistently)* There are.

*(*MIRANDA *frowns.)*

YASMIN: For example. There is a superhero in New York City who patrols the streets outside night clubs late at night, protecting women who have had too much to drink from ending up the prey of men. There is a superhero in Britain who cuts off wheel clamps from cars. There is a superhero in Canada who shovels off the snow from sidewalks and protects the streets at night from crime. There is a superhero in Mexico City who uses his name and costume to campaign about corruption and crime. Hardly anyone knows these men and women's true identities beyond their masks but these real life superhero's *are there* nonetheless.

MIRANDA: But these aren't *real* superheroes, are they, Yasmin? They're just slightly odd men and women wearing masks and with good intentions. Do you see the difference?

(YASMIN *frowns. She sighs.*)

YASMIN: *(Finally)* Look. Are you going to help me or not?

(MIRANDA *hesitates.*)

YASMIN: Because I've got a lot to do.

(MIRANDA *hesitates.*)

YASMIN: What with saving the world and all.

(MIRANDA *hesitates.*)

YASMIN: I need to...know what to wear for a start— a superhero has to have a costume.

(MIRANDA *hesitates.*)

YASMIN: Then I need to know what to think— a superhero has to have a moral code, otherwise the costume is just superfluous.

(MIRANDA *hesitates.*)

YASMIN: I need to know how to disguise myself— I'll need flexibility—I'll need to be able to get out of school when necessary and I'm hoping I can count on you for a sick note.

(MIRANDA *frowns.*)

YASMIN: Superheroes also sometimes have a sidekick, so if you like, you could be my Robin.

(MIRANDA *frowns harder.*)

MIRANDA: Yasmin—

YASMIN: What? Do you know that female superheroes are usually weak and poorly drawn and primarily love interests? I look at this as a great opportunity to right those wrongs for both of us.

MIRANDA: Yasmin—

YASMIN: Oh, and I need an evil nemesis but we can work that out later.

MIRANDA: YASMIN.

YASMIN: *(Hesitating)* What? My Mum told me you'd help me. Right?

MIRANDA: *(Slowly)* Yes. *(She thinks.)* Yes. That's right.

(She smiles at YASMIN.*)*

MIRANDA: Your Mum's doing much better, actually. *(She smiles again.)* It's great she's got a new job.

*(*YASMIN *doesn't reply.)*

MIRANDA: She tells me you're doing terrifically well at school too.

*(*YASMIN *doesn't reply.)*

MIRANDA: A straight A student.

*(*YASMIN *doesn't reply.)*

MIRANDA: You must be very proud of you both.

YASMIN: *(Impatiently)* Look, I don't...want to talk about that now. Not when I've got saving the world to think about. You're my mother's doctor. I'm trusting you with this. Will you help me or not?

MIRANDA: Yes... Yes. I will. *(She hesitates.)* If this happens again.

*(*YASMIN *pauses, unsure.* MIRANDA *smiles at* YASMIN.*)*

MIRANDA: I think you have a wonderful imagination, Yasmin. Embrace it. Relax. *(She smiles.)* Come back and see me again next week.

(She continues to smile. She writes something down on a piece of paper. She hands it to YASMIN. YASMIN *looks at the paper blankly.)*

YASMIN: *(Reading)* "One anti-flying prescription for Yasmin".

(She looks up at MIRANDA.*)*

YASMIN: Why would I need that?

*(*MIRANDA *shrugs.)*

MIRANDA: Sometimes you need to remember to keep your feet on the ground, Yasmin...I'll see you next week.

(Lights fade.)

Scene Three

*(*YASMIN, *to the audience)*

YASMIN: With my imaginary prescription in hand, I make my way back to school in time for General Studies, where an in-depth discussion of "world disasters" such as New Orleans, the war in Iraq and the bombings in London, is in full swing. Admittedly, by "full swing" I mean that my teacher is talking, impassioned and oblivious, at the front of the class whilst my classmates whisper to each other, pass notes, and attempt to poke the fat boy who sits in the front row with pencils they are surreptitiously launching from under their desks, but this being school anything that isn't either silence or detention inducing chaos counts for "full swing", believe me. When I enter the room, late and red-faced and filled with secret excitement about my new super-human strengths, Mrs

Reid turns to me with relief and smiles and says loudly
"Well, I know *you* will have prepared something for
class, Yasmin," which is why no one likes me and
I have to sit at the front next to the fat boy, being
occasionally hit by pencils which stray from their
course.

   Unfortunately, instead of telling Mrs Reid that my
having prepared something for class will lead to several
pencils "accidentally" going off course, my mother has
brought me up well and so I smile and say "yes, I have
prepared something for class" and I throw my bag
down on my desk and I pull out my notebook and I
stand at my desk, telling my class how random I find
everything to be. How one day you get on the tube and
you happen to sit down next to a suicide bomber who is
about to trigger his device and how I can't see what you
can do about that. How one day you go to work and
you happen to have gotten your new job, your work to
make money, the day before in the World Trade Center
and how I can't see what you can do about that. How
you happen to have been born in Iraq or Palestine or
Afghanistan or the Sudan and you want to be a doctor
but instead you end up in the line outside the police
station or in a market or on a bus at the wrong moment
and how I can't see what you can do about that.
And how this is making me so sad and panicked or
something because I don't understand why the news is
showing us these images when there's *nothing*, there's
absolutely nothing you can do about these things, it
doesn't matter if you've led a good life or bad, if you've
put others first nor not, if you have dreams unfulfilled
or not, if you happen to be in the wrong place that's it,
and there's nothing any of us can do about that.

   And, as I am talking, and my classmates are rolling
their eyes and passing notes and my teacher is
frowning, because this isn't the kind of impassioned
tone she was hoping for, I begin to feel myself lift off

the ground. And so I stop talking and I begin panicking, because it's one thing to bore your classmates with a speech and quite another to *actually take off in public* (This never happened to Clark Kent and for a moment it passes through my mind to ask why there isn't a phone box for me) and, anyway, the more I panic the higher I rise until finally I am flailing around in the air several inches above the desks.

At this point, my teacher falls into a dead faint and collapses onto the floor, which unusual event attracts my classmates' attention long enough for them to notice that I am currently suspended in mid-air.

For a moment, there is a silence, an armistice I like to think, as my classmates and I eye each other in mutual contemplation, I from my place near the ceiling, they from their place on the ground.

And then it comes.

OHMYGODTHEFUCKINGFREAK.

(A long moment. YASMIN *looks around her. Lights fade.)*

Scene Four

*(*MIRANDA, *working at her desk.* YASMIN *enters. She is wearing a torn home-made superhero costume and is bloodied and bruised.)*

YASMIN: *(Hesitantly)* So. I guess my disguise is ruined then.

*(*MIRANDA *raises her eyebrows.)*

MIRANDA: You think?

*(*YASMIN *looks at* MIRANDA *blankly.)*

YASMIN: Why are you such a bitch?

*(*MIRANDA *flinches.)*

YASMIN: I blame you of course.

(MIRANDA *frowns.*)

YASMIN: You're the doctor.

(MIRANDA *frowns harder.*)

YASMIN: You're the adult.

(MIRANDA *hesitates.*)

YASMIN: You're meant to protect me from this.

MIRANDA: Did I tell you to go into school wearing a superhero costume, Yasmin?

(YASMIN *shrugs.*)

MIRANDA: Did I tell you to tie yourself to the railings outside of school, Yamsin?

(YASMIN *shrugs.*)

MIRANDA: Did I tell you to let your classmates beat you?

(YASMIN *frowns.*)

YASMIN: A superhero only ever uses his or her superpowers for good.

MIRANDA: For god's sake. You're *not* a superhero, Yasmin. This has gone far enough.

YASMIN: How can you say that?

MIRANDA: Because it's true. There is no such thing as superheroes in this world.

YASMIN: But I am one.

MIRANDA: YOU'RE NOT.

(*Beat*)

YASMIN: I am.

(MIRANDA *sighs.*)

MIRANDA: O K. Then prove it.

(YASMIN *hesitates.*)

MIRANDA: Show me.

(YASMIN *hesitates.*)

MIRANDA: Show me.

(YASMIN *hesitates.*)

MIRANDA: Show me how you can fly.

(YASMIN *hesitates. After a moment, she closes her eyes. She concentrates. A pause. She opens her eyes.*)

YASMIN: I can't.

MIRANDA: *(Triumphantly)* Exactly.

YASMIN: But just because I can't show you at this precise moment, it doesn't mean I'm not a superhero, it just means I'm not a performing puppet -

MIRANDA: Doesn't it?

YASMIN: No. I can prove it.

(*She picks up her school bag from the floor. She pulls out a long ceremonial military sword.* MIRANDA *stands up from her desk in alarm.*)

MIRANDA: Where did you get that?

YASMIN: It was my father's. He was in the army. He left it when he left us. It's for defeating my enemies now. *(She hesitates.)* Like She-Ra's sword.

MIRANDA: I'm not your enemy, Yasmin.

YASMIN: Aren't you?

MIRANDA: No.

(YASMIN *looks at* MIRANDA. *She looks at the sword. She smiles. She puts the sword back into her bag.*)

YASMIN: *(Frowning)* Even if you were, I wouldn't use this on you. Superhero's never kill an enemy, even at the expense of their own safety.

(MIRANDA smiles.)

YASMIN: Although, since the late 1970s, there have been exceptions to this rule. Wolverine, The Punisher—
(She hesitates.)
But they've never really taken off.
(She paces the room.) So. What do you think I should do now that my cover is blown?

MIRANDA: *(Slowly)* I think you should come and see me and a colleague tomorrow, Yasmin, with your Mum. We'll sort it out. Together. I promise.

(Beat. YASMIN looks at MIRANDA.)

YASMIN: Like the X-Men?

(MIRANDA looks blank.)

YASMIN: They're a group of superheroes.

(MIRANDA looks at YASMIN. She doesn't smile.)

MIRANDA: Just come back tomorrow, Yasmin. Please.

Scene Five

(MIRANDA, apparently to the audience)

MIRANDA: Superman was born in the 1930s to Jewish American parents. He grew up in depression era America. During the Second World War, he found himself to be extremely popular thanks to the charming and hopeful escapades of his youth. Then, in the 1950s, his popularity began to wane. After the end of the war, the world no longer had a need for him for you a while, you see.
(She hesitates.)
I'm saying. What am I saying? I'm saying. That I'm concerned why Yasmin has a need for these superheros. That's all.
(She hesitates.)

Because I had a need for a superhero when I was six,
you see. And it wasn't healthy. It really wasn't.
It wasn't a stable career choice or stable life choice.
People say that being in the medical profession is
sometimes underpaid and overworked. Well, that's
nothing compared to being a superhero, believe me.
(She laughs.)
I'm sorry. I know that's not funny. I joke when I'm
nervous. I apologise.
(She frowns.)
I'm just saying. That carrying a sword is not normal
behaviour. By anyone's standards. It's not something
I can fix with a prescription. "Do not kill anyone,
Yasmin" or a "normal" pill. I wish I could. I wish there
was such a thing as a normal pill. But there's not. Look.
You don't need to take this personally. This has no
reflection on you as a mother. I swear. Because we all
need superheroes. But there's a difference between
needing and *needing*. Isn't there? You're a good mother
to Yasmin. I'm sure you'll understand what we need to
do now.

(Lights fade.)

Scene Six

(YASMIN, to the audience.)

YASMIN: When I get back to school, filled with
light hearted and headed relief after my successful
assignation at the doctor's, I arrive to find the entire
school has gathered in the playground. They turn to
me as I approach and then hastily turn away again
when they see that it is only me. And so I follow their
eyes until I see what they are all looking at.
(She hesitates.)
And, so, this is how I find myself looking at my mother.
She is standing on the roof of the school, balancing

from what I can see, precariously on the gutter just
above the science block and gesturing that we should
all go away. And, as I draw nearer, I ask Mrs Reid, who
happens to be one of the closest and keenest observers,
how I can get up to the roof, and she shushes me,
saying, "Not now, Yasmin, I'm watching this lady,
I don't have time for this now" and her eyes never leave
my mother's face.
And suddenly it all makes sense. I know what I have
to do. I know what I can do. And because I can do this,
I suddenly feel O K.
And so I look up at my mother.
At her pale face.
Her wobbly knees.
Her profusely sweating forehead.
And
Very slowly
I make my way towards the roof
And
As my mother jumps
I close my eyes
And we fly.

(Lights fade on YASMIN.*)*

(Lights momentarily rise on MIRANDA, *working at her desk.
She looks up for a moment from her work, troubled by some
uncertain thought. She pauses. After a moment, she shakes
her head, clearing it. She returns to her work. Lights fade.)*

AFTER THE FLOOD
Dorothy Fortenberry

CHARACTERS & SETTING

ALTHEA, *African-American, from Louisiana, forties*
TOM, *white, from Virginia, thirties*
LUCILLE, *white, from Louisiana, thirties*
ROSE, *African-American, from Louisiana thirties*
ANNETTE, *white, from Louisiana, forties*
PATRICK, *white, from New York City, twenties*
SARAH, *African-American, from Louisiana, eighties*
SISTER CLARICE, *white, from Ohio, twenties*
HERBERT, *white, from Iowa, fifties*
MICHELLE, *white, Cajun, eighteen*
TIBBY, *African-American, from Louisiana, fourteen*
SUZANNE, *white, from Louisiana, twenties*

*Note: This play can be performed with five actors (two
African-American women, two white women, one white
man.)* ALTHEA *is played by one actor.* ROSE, SARAH, *and*
TIBBY *are played by one actor.* LUCILLE *and* MICHELLE *are
played by one actor.* ANNETTE, SISTER CLARICE, *and*
SUZANNE *are played by one actor.* TOM, PATRICK, *and*
HERBERT *are played by one actor.*

Time: from April, 1926 through September, 1927

Place: Louisiana

SCENES

1. FLOOD

ALTHEA: Good Friday is the day that Jesus was nailed to the cross. Always struck me as a little strange to call it Good Friday. But then again, I don't come up with the names. This year, Good Friday was even less good than usual. It's been raining fierce since August, ruining my family's crops, messing with our health, and most of all, making the river rise. By Mardi Gras, we knew what was coming, we just didn't know when. Then, on April 15, 1927—Good Friday—we got the largest and heaviest storm of all. It was the beginning of the Flood.

2. LEVEES-ONLY POLICY "THE BEST WAY TO GO"
(Baton Rouge, April, 1926)

TOM: Gentlemen of the Mississippi River Commission, Senator Broussard, Congressmen, and distinguished guests and colleagues, I am here today on behalf of the Army Corps of Engineers to discuss our excellent system of river containment and river control. Now, as many of you know, we here at the Corps follow what is known as a levees-only policy. Employing the most advanced scientific techniques available, we have determined that the best way to control the mighty Mississippi is to force its water to move fast and go deep. In a typical flood, with no levees, water spreads out to the sides, creating more floods and more damage. But thanks to our levees-only policy, we keep that river contained. It moves faster and instead of spreading sideways, it digs deeper, flowing straight into the sea. Same amount of water, mind you, no flood. I'm sure all of you remember four years ago, the flood of 1922. We at the Army Corps of Engineers are proud to remind you that for the first time in history, thanks to our levees-only system, a Mississippi River flood passed all the way from Illinois to the Gulf of Mexico without a single break in a levee. A levee built to the standards of the Mississippi River Commission, that is. For those of you interested in the science behind all this, when we talk about floods, we use a term called second-feet, which is the average speed of the river's current multiplied by the area of the river itself. For example, in a spot on the river that's a thousand feet wide and ten feet deep—.

ALTHEA: When the flood comes, twenty-seven thousand square miles will be inundated. 931,159 people will be homeless. Economic losses from the flood will approach one million dollars. The official death toll will be two hundred and forty-six.

TOM: But this is a lot of facts and figures, gentlemen. I don't want to make your heads swim. At the end of the day, all you really need to know is this—.

ALTHEA: All you really need to know is this—.

TOM: Those levees are safe and our system is sound.

3. HAVE YOU BEEN SAVED?
(Ville Platte, May, 1927)

LUCILLE: Good morning everyone, and what a fine morning it is. Now, this fine morning my husband has asked me to come and preach before you today, and Reverend, I thank you. You, sir, you see that the truth of the Lord Jesus burns in my soul as it does in yours and I am just honored and blessed that you trust me to share the Word with all these wonderful people out here. And, wonderful people, I thank you, too, I thank you for coming to this meeting to hear the Word and for taking it out and sharing it with your friends and your families when you leave. Now, I know many of you must have heard this week's news about the levee. How many of you, can I get a show of hands, how many of you heard that news? Mmm-hmm. And how many of you felt sorry for those people? Yet another town along the Mississippi flooded, more people without homes, is that right? Did you feel sorry for them? Did you? Well, let me tell you something, you can just stop that sorryness right now. Jesus does not want you to feel sorry for those people. He wants to you understand that they are being punished, and that you, too, will be punished, you, too, will watch your wife and children wash away down a river. Jesus says so himself, right here in Matthew, Chapter 7, Verse 24:

ALTHEA: "Therefore, whosoever heareth these sayings of mine, and doeth them, I will liken him unto a wise man, which built his house upon a rock: And the rain descended, and the floods came, and the winds blew, and beat upon that house; and it fell not: for it was founded upon a rock."

LUCILLE: That's what happened to me. We live outside Natchitoches, and the rains have been coming, but did our house fall? No. It was founded upon the rock of our faith. But what about the people you've been hearing about, those people you've been feeling sorry for, what does Jesus have to say about them?

ALTHEA: "And every one that heareth these sayings of mine, and doeth them not, shall be likened unto a foolish man, which built his house upon the sand: And the rain descended, and the floods came, and the winds blew, and beat upon that house; and it fell: and great was the fall of it."

LUCILLE: Amen. Do you think it's just a coincidence that the floods only happen in the most Catholic areas of our country? Does it flood in Alabama? No. Georgia? No. Only right here in Louisiana, where the faithless and the wicked are being swept to the sea. So many people ask me, Lucille, they say, what is my responsibility to the people who have suffered in this flood? How can I help? Do you know what I say? I say your responsibility to people who have suffered in this flood is to think about your own salvation. How can you help? By getting right with God. And once you're born again, you go out and you find someone and you help save him. That's the only way to stop these tragedies: build your house upon the solid rock of Jesus Christ.

ALTHEA: Amen.

4. RED CROSS DELIVERS AID TO VICTIMS
(Camp, June 1927)

ROSE: Time for dinner everybody. Get your bowls.

ALTHEA: She's at the camp canteen today, getting her rations from the Red Cross ladies. Rice. Beans. Canned milk for the children.

(ROSE *takes a bowl and stands in line, waiting to receive food*)

ROSE: I know it's the same as last night, but it's food, isn't it?

ALTHEA: Most days the meals here are the same, rice, beans, cornmeal. What they call soup. Dished out, one spoonful per person, and carefully guarded so nobody can sneak in there and steal more than his share. No tables, no chairs, no spoons, just a bowl, and a place in the mud to squat and eat.

ROSE: Fine, you don't like it, you don't have to eat it, but there's no need to talk like that.

ALTHEA: But today there's something different. She notices it as she waits in the line, listening in on the conversations around her, trying to figure out if anyone has news—about when they can leave, about what's happened to the land, about family still missing. She sees peaches, canned peaches, just arrived.

ROSE: Where's your sister? Did she wander off again? Go get her, would you—I can't be getting out of line.

ALTHEA: She asks,

ROSE: What about the peaches? Can I have some of those? I got kids at home. You can look it up.

ALTHEA: But they say no.

ROSE: My husband's got his job tag on like he's supposed to. He's out there working on the levee right—.

ALTHEA: No again. And as she walks out, she hears one of the Red Cross ladies say:

ANNETTE: Peaches. If they got accustomed to peaches here, just think how spoiled they'd be once they left. It's for their own good; that's what it is. Isn't that right?

5. NAMES MAKE NEWS
(Thibodeaux, May, 1927 to Lucille)

PATRICK: Look, lady, I've been to church before.

ALTHEA: He went every day. He tried and failed and every next day he tried again to live the life God wanted him to. And he knew the nuns were trying and failing and the priests were trying and failing, but he thought, maybe if he tried hard enough, maybe he could get it right.

PATRICK: I know Scripture. I know Matthew—Chapter 25? About Jesus coming back to judge us? I know what we're supposed to do.

ALTHEA: "I was hungry and you gave me food, I was thirsty and you gave me drink, I was a stranger and you welcomed me...as you did it to one of the least of these my brethren, you did it to me."

PATRICK: Damn right I know it.

ALTHEA: He tried it. He tried to see his parents as Jesus, neighbors, children, bums on the street. To look into their eyes and see God, come back to earth to test him. He left his neighborhood for a rougher one and a rougher one, seeking out the most miserable because they were most likely to be Christ, until he was living in filth and he started, well, to crack up. His parents found him, eventually, brought him back home, made him finish high school. They screwed his head back on straight, got one of the priests to talk to him about moderation. And he got this job. Newspaperman. And he's back in the misery, up to his neck in it, but this time, he doesn't see Jesus' face. He sees his editor's, his publisher's. He's got papers to sell, and sometimes suffering does the trick.

PATRICK: Thing is, you'd be amazed how much people like this flood story. All over the country I've got people buying my stuff. Did they catch the guy stealing the relief supplies? Why hasn't President Coolidge been here once? What's next for Hoover, the "Great Humanitarian?" And pictures—the river wide as the land, or the sea. Big stories like that, but little ones, too, just the right degree of sad. Cute little girl separated from her family, taken in by kindly strangers. And pets—people love the goddamn drowning pets. And the more I see of people, the more I think that nothing—

ALTHEA: Not Jesus not anybody

PATRICK: Is going to get them—us—to be anything other than whores. Beg your pardon. Jesus came back to earth today, the best thing I could do is sell him a paper. Or, maybe, get him to take out an advertisement. So, no, ma'am, no, I have not accepted Christ as my personal savior. I don't think I'll attend your tent revival this evening. But thank you so much for asking.

6. LOST AND FOUND
(May, 1927)

SARAH: Here, Buddy! Buddy! *(Pause)* Goddamn it Buddy, would you just paddle on over here? *(Pause)* He'd always come when I called him.

ALTHEA: He'd never come when she called him.

SARAH: Ever since that first day when I took him from my sister's house after she passed on. Her kids didn't want him, but I said I wouldn't mind a companion. He was sad then, but he got happy as soon as he saw he was coming to live with me. Just started wagging his stumpy little tail and drooling right and left. He's medium-sized

ALTHEA: Small.

SARAH: Golden.

ALTHEA: Brown.

SARAH: And he's a very good swimmer. *(Pause)* Buddy! Buddy!

7. OUR LADY OF GOOD COUNSEL
(New Orleans, May, 1927)

SISTER CLARICE: Hello, everyone, welcome. I am so glad to see all of you here; I know most of you would probably rather be somewhere else, but here you are, and here I am. *(Pause.)* What I mean is, even though we were brought here by misfortune, there is still so much to appreciate, isn't there? Just that we're here, right now, together, is, in its own way, a miracle. I know that's got to be hard to believe, but even in the midst of sorrow, there is room for gratitude, if only for our lives and a roof over our heads. I'm sorry, I haven't even—. I'm Sister Clarice.

ALTHEA: She's new here. She's come down specially to New Orleans from Ohio to help out here at Our Lady of Good Counsel.

SISTER CLARICE: And I look forward to getting to know each and every one of you.

ALTHEA: She believes, and she wants you to believe, despite, and perhaps even because of what you've been through, that you are blessed. Truly blessed. Each and every one of you is, and she's sorry she doesn't know your names yet, but each and every one of you is a beloved child of God.

SISTER CLARICE: Tonight we're going to be praying the rosary, and yes, I know some of you were asking, we will be serving dinner afterward. If anyone still hasn't signed in with Sister Assumptia, please do so. She's by the pile of blankets over in the rectory. It's really best if you sign in with her; that way we can keep track of who's here.

ALTHEA: Also, Sister Assumptia hands out the diapers.

SISTER CLARICE: The rosary. I think tonight, there's a special intercession to make to Mary, and I invite you all to join me. We pray to her tonight to ask her Son to extend His generous hand to all of us here in Louisiana. To the sick, the dying, the homeless, to ease our suffering and grant us peace. Now, if everyone could take out her beads—if you don't have beads, we have some extra up here—and begin. In the name of the Father, and the Son, and the Holy Spirit. Amen

ALTHEA: I believe in God, the Father Almighty, creator of Heaven and Earth... *(She continues rosary into beginning of next scene.)*

8. THE GREAT HUMANITARIAN
(New Orleans, July, 1927)

HERBERT: Good afternoon, Rotarians of New Orleans. Thank you for welcoming me to your beautiful city. As I have traveled throughout this region, monitoring the remarkable progress that we are making in our relief effort, I have to say that nothing impresses me more than the American volunteer spirit. I see it in churches, in the Red Cross, and in this very organization. I see it in every association committed to helping the victims of this disaster. And I applaud you. Now, I know some of you must have questions about how our relief effort is proceeding, and I would be happy to answer them.

ALTHEA: In April, President Calvin Coolidge placed commerce Secretary Herbert Hoover in charge of the flood effort. Secretary Hoover was in the Midwest and South as the flood spread, and he organized the federal response. President Coolidge did not visit the afflicted areas himself.

HERBERT: I'm glad you asked me that. The President and I have a very close relationship, and agree

completely on how this relief effort should be handled.
He gave me the authority to coordinate fundraising and
distribution, and I have to say, he is as pleased as I am
with the results.

ALTHEA: Congress was on recess during the flood
and not scheduled to meet again until January, 1928.
Certain members of both parties and several national
newspapers pushed for a special session of Congress
in which to appropriate money for flood victims, but
President Coolidge did not call one. He and Secretary
Hoover believed a special session of Congress was not
needed.

HERBERT: Well, it's very kind of you say that, sir. And I
certainly agree with you: a special session of Congress
at this time is simply unnecessary. Local organizations
are doing a tremendous job of everything that's
asked of them, without handouts from the federal
government. For example, when we've got a couple
thousand people coming to a camp, I tell the local
committee what needs to be done: huts, watermains,
sewers, streets, dining halls, meals, doctors. Everything.
They simply go ahead and do it.

ALTHEA: This year, the government collected a record
surplus. Six hundred thirty-five million dollars. Not
a cent of federal money will go in direct aid to flood
victims. For forks, shoes, chairs, medicines, combs,
shirts, beds.

HERBERT: Now, that's a tricky one. I suppose I was just
blessed with a good upbringing and education. But,
really, the credit doesn't belong to me, it belongs to you.
It belongs to the thirty thousand Red Cross volunteers.
It belongs to the Elks, the Masons, the American
Legion, and the Junior League. It belongs to the tens
of millions of men, women, and children across the
country who personally made a donation to the cause.
It is a success based in the extraordinary resilience and

generosity of the American people. Some folks, these days, find it fashionable to demean our small towns, but I say they are the heart of all that is good. We rescued Main Street with Main Street. The cooperative spirit of Main Street is what is putting the Mississippi Valley back on its feet after the flood. The people of the valley are settling their own problems of rehabilitation without a great deal of outside help. It is upon such independence and self-government that is based the greatness of the United States.

9. LOUISIANA LEVEE CUT TO MAKE NEW ORLEANS SAFE
(Camp, June, 1927 to Patrick)

MICHELLE: You've seen the chickens, haven't you? I mean there's mules and cows, too, and dogs, but the thing that gets me most is the chickens, just bobbing along on the surface of the river, like they were ducks, like they were swimming almost. Anyway, that's how I feel. Like a chicken. You going to write that down? Good. Bwak-bwak. That's my chicken noise. Hey, hey, you know what's funny? When we showed up here and we said, we lost our house, we lost everything we have, they gave us packets of seeds. *(Pause)* Seeds, right? They said, "God helps those that helps themselves" and they handed us the seeds, like we could plant a vegetable garden right there in the mud and have food in time for dinner. I was already feeling like a chicken, just floating along with nothing, and when they handed us the packet, I turned to my brother Rober, and I said, "Looks like we must be chickens, they've given us chicken feed." Well, he thought it was funny.

ALTHEA: They're river rats. That's what folks call them around here. Because they work on the river. Roger works—worked—as a trapper. Their house had stilts, for when the river rose, but stilts only go so far up. They're from Saint Bernard parish, so they knew their house would get flooded. They even knew what day. When the most powerful businessmen in New Orleans decided to dynamite the Saint Bernard levee to spare their city—not that New Orleans was liable to flood, it wasn't—they promised all the people who'd lose their homes "full compensation." And then those businessmen and their families had a party on the banks of the levee, eating sandwiches, and taking photographs of the dynamite. Most folks are still waiting to be compensated. They're going to be waiting a long time.

MICHELLE: Hey—you want to hear a joke? Here's a Boudreaux story—you know about Boudreaux stories? Well, this is one. Boudreaux, he's drunk, right, and Sunday after the flood, he ends up at a baptism that's happening down by the river. He walks down into the water and stands next to the preacher. The preacher turns and notices him all drunk and says, "Mister, are you ready to find Jesus?" And Boudreaux says, "Yes, I sure am!" So he dunks Boudreaux under the water and pulls him right back up. "Have you found Jesus?" he asks. "No, I sure didn't!" Boudreaux says. Then the preacher dunks him under for a little bit longer, brings him up and says, "Now, brother, have you found Jesus?" And Boudreaux says "No, I sure didn't!" Finally, the preacher holds Boudreaux under for a good two minutes, brings him out of the water and says to him, "My good man, have you found Jesus yet?" And Boudreaux wipes his eyes and he says to the preacher, "Are you sure this is where he fell in?"

10. KINDLY STRANGERS
(Amite, August, 1927)

TIBBY: Don't you try to pity me, woman, don't you dare. I can see it right there, in your raised eyebrows, the cock of your head, the clasped palms, the unnecessary use of "honey," "darling" "sugar." Fuck that. I don't want to talk about it. I won't want to talk about it. I promise you, I guarantee, I will never ever in a million years want to talk to you about it, cross my heart and hope to die and I mean it. You want to test me? Fine. Test me. I can wait you out easy. Go.

You know what I don't understand, one of the many, millions of things I don't understand—why in the hell they won't just let me live alone? You'd think enough had happened to me—

ALTHEA: That having both her parents and her baby brother die in the flood would be enough to be left alone.

TIBBY: I can take care of myself—hell, I am taking care of myself, so why won't you let me be already? Jesus. "Kindly strangers" that's what they called you in the paper. I read the story, saw the picture. They put my hair in fucking pigtails in that picture. I don't wear pigtails. I haven't worn pigtails since I was maybe eight years old, but there I am, in pigtails holding your hand and looking shy. I am not shy. *(Pause)* And if you think I'm calling you Mama Ann, you better think again and quick. I had a Mama once. Now I—. Look, just because you're all dried up on the inside and can't ever have real babies of your own, that don't mean you're going to get me to call you Mama.

And you lie, too. I know you do. You ask me, leaving your wrinkly-ass hand on mine one second too long in the morning over eggs—I hate eggs, my real Mama

knew that—you ask me "do I want to talk about it?"
but you don't really mean it. You don't really want to
know. I know the story you want to hear, the happy
story where you're the fairy godmother who saved
me and shit. But you don't really want to know.

ALTHEA: To know that she watched them die in front
of her, because she happened to catch a piece of wood
floating along, and so she lived and they died. She saw
her Daddy sink and her Mama's skirt swirl over her
head in the river, leaving her exposed as she floated
on by. That it was so simple, watching Johnny drown,
so peaceful, it didn't even seem like a bad thing—or
about how long she lay on that piece of wood in the
dark, and how after a certain period of time, she
couldn't think anymore, all she could do was count.
One Mississippi, two Mississippi. She got all the way
up to seven thousand three hundred and twenty-one
Mississippi. And instead of sleeping each night, she
keeps on counting Mississippis because she can't sleep
and she's afraid she never will.

TIBBY: You don't want any of it. So I don't give it to you.
You want to pity me, so you can feel good about
yourself and how kindly a stranger you are. Good luck.
And I will never even once let you see me cry.

11. LAST STAND FIGHT MAY DEFEAT FLOOD
(Saint Francisville, April, 1927)

ALTHEA: It had been raining every night for months
and it kept raining afterwards, too, but something
about that night was special. They knew, even from the
moment they got home that this wasn't just ordinary,
all-the-time rain. Folks had been talking for weeks
about the possibility of the levee busting. Further up
the river, clear on up to Cairo and Columbus, levees
had been exploding, and they said that any day now,

the levee here at Saint Francisville could go. All it would take was one last heavy rainstorm. So that night, when the rain came, they knew what they were supposed to do. They knew, she and Walter, that they were supposed to take his gun and her necklace, a suitcase of clothes and as much food as they could carry, and go to higher ground, wait in a church, or a school till the rain passed. And they considered it, briefly, on their own. This is what they should do. It would be a good idea. But as soon as the rain started getting hard, she knew they weren't going anywhere.

SUZANNE: Our house has a tin roof, Walter put it up there himself, and when it rains hard, you can hear every drop hit that roof, and, I like that sound, I like hearing it in bed and he likes hearing me when I'm hearing it. They say, during heavy rainstorms, there's electricity in the air, you can measure it, and I believe it because when I reach out my hand to touch Walter, I get a shock—blue, you can see it in the dark. And we stand there, our faces barely visible, but glowing a little, and I reach out my hand again. And again. I keep touching him and touching him, telling him I want to see the electricity, and he touches me back. When he kisses me, he pulls my hair, hard, the way I like it, and after he lifts his hand, my hair is all whichways with the static. We run upstairs, me chasing Walter, slapping his ass and then we fall on the bed and he tries to rip my shirt off, pulling on my breasts, but the fabric won't break and I start giggling and he rolls me over on my stomach and lifts the shirt clear over my head. We're listening to the sound of the raindrops like buckshot on our roof, feeling the wind push our walls in, seeing each other's bodies bright in flashes of lightning. I sit up and grab his belt and pull it out of his pants and he takes it from my hand, smiling, and I know he means to use it. Then he grabs me and pulls me on his lap and we're sitting on the edge of the bed. He reaches around

and touches me right when the thunder sounds, and I
breathe fast, faster, and close my eyes until I'm right on
the edge and as I open them, I explode.

12. AFTERMATH
(Camp, September, 1927)

ALTHEA: Good evening, brothers and sisters. We're here
tonight to talk about Noah. It seemed only appropriate
with what all has been going on recently, to spend some
time with a man who knows his way around a flood.
Now, I know you know the story of Noah, every child
who goes to Sunday School knows the story of Noah,
but I want to talk about Noah tonight all the same. It
says, in the Good Book, that Noah was a just man and
perfect in his generation and that Noah walked with
God. And I want you all to ask yourselves, "Do I walk
with God? Does my family walk with God?" And do
the men and women I see each day, the men and
women who tell us where to go and what to do, who
dole out rations and work orders and everything but
permission to leave, the people who rounded up our
men and made them lay their bodies in piles across the
levees to keep back the flood—do they walk with God?
I want you to think about that.
    As you know, Noah was commanded by God to build
an ark; he built this ark and filled it with his family and
two of every kind of beast—the cattle, the fowl, the
creeping things and the things that fly. And Noah
sealed up the ark and it started to rain. It rained for
forty days and forty nights. You know, when I was a
little girl, and I heard that, I thought it was such a long
time. But forty days and forty nights? That's nothing.
Now, it does say that the waters prevailed on the earth
for a hundred and fifty days, but I've already been here
for three months with no sign that anyone's going to

pay me back for my house that was lost, for my
belongings, for what was taken from me. So a hundred
and fifty days? In an ark? Doesn't seem so bad right
now.

Noah, he lived on that ark for a hundred and fifty
days with the animals and his family until the waters
started to recede. And when they made it to land, he
gave a burnt offering to the Lord, who saw it and who
promised "I will not again curse the ground any more
for man's sake." He said "Neither shall all flesh be cut
off any more by the waters of a flood; neither shall there
any more be a flood to destroy the earth."

That's what He said, and He put a rainbow in the sky
as a mark of His promise. So that whenever He looked
at it, the Lord would remember His promise to His
people on earth.

Well.

You know, when I was preparing myself for tonight,
and I considered the rainbow, I had two thoughts, and
I'd like to share them with you. My first thought was
that I haven't seen a rainbow in a long, long time. I got
to thinking that it was just raining so much that there
wasn't room for a rainbow to appear. That maybe the
Lord forgot about us for a little bit and that's why He
sent another flood. That it was as if the piece of string
He tied around His majestic finger had fallen off,
and the promise just slipped His mind. That we better
find an artificial rainbow machine, and fast, so we can
produce bright, beautiful rainbows every day so that
He won't forget us, what with all the other things He's
busy worrying about. That was my first thought.

But then I got to thinking about why. Why did the
Good Lord send the flood in the first place? Why did
He decide to obliterate almost all His creation?

Well.

According to Genesis, in the time of Noah, the earth
was corrupt. That's why He had to send that flood,

because the earth was corrupt before Him and filled with violence. That's why He did it. And I want you to ask yourself, "is my world corrupt? Do I see a world corrupt with violence?" Ask yourself that question, my brothers and sisters. Ask yourself.

WAYS YOU CAN SURVIVE THE WORLD
PART TWO: FIND JESUS
Jennifer Tuckett

CHARACTERS & SETTING

KATIE, *aged twelve*
MARY, KATIE's *mother.*

The set should be minimal and does not need to be realistic.

Scene One

(MARY, *to the audience*)

MARY: I want to believe that there is a God worth believing in.

Two months ago, my husband was killed in a road accident driving home from work. He was speeding in order to reach home before my daughter Katie's bedtime. It was a senseless and pointless loss but Katie and I have strengthened our hearts to go on.

Yesterday morning, my daughter came downstairs for breakfast and she said to me "Mummy, I am recovering from my father's death. Today, I feel happy for the first time," and I wanted to go down on my knees and say "thank you, God. Thank you for giving my child the strength to regain her innocence."

And then Katie said to me, "the reason I feel better, Mummy, is because I have become Jesus Christ in the night. I woke up this morning and I knew that I was Jesus Christ reborn and this made me so happy, it really did."

(She looks at the audience.)

I want to believe that there is a God worth believing in, but sometimes the world makes this really fucking hard.

(Light fades.)

Scene Two

(KATIE, *to the audience*)

KATIE: I am Jesus Christ. Basically, the realisation that I am Jesus Christ came to me surprisingly easily. I woke up one morning and suddenly it all made sense. My mother is called Mary. My father was a furniture restorer, which is pretty close to being a carpenter, right? And I have been in the wilderness for a long time, and I have survived.

And I was so happy when I realised that I was Jesus Christ. Really. I was.

(MARY *enters.*)

MARY: You're not Jesus Christ, Katie.

KATIE: You're just saying that. Because you're not religious.

MARY: No. I'm saying that because it's not true.

KATIE: But think how great it would be if you did believe that I was Jesus Christ.

MARY: Katie—

KATIE: The evil people would be punished.

MARY: Katie—

KATIE: The just rewarded—

MARY: Katie—

KATIE: The dead would rise again—

MARY: I think that's Frankenstein not Jesus, Katie.

KATIE: No, it's Jesus. I'm telling you.

(MARY *takes* KATIE *by the shoulders. She looks at her steadily.*)

MARY: You are not Jesus Christ.

(KATIE is silent.)

MARY: There is no Jesus Christ.

(KATIE is silent.)

MARY: There is no God.

(KATIE is silent.)

MARY: If there was a God, your father would not be dead.

(KATIE is silent.)

MARY: If there was a God, you and I would not be alone.

(KATIE is silent.)

MARY: If there was a God, I would not have an imbecile for a daughter just when I needed her most.

(She shakes KATIE violently.)

MARY: Do you hear what I am saying, Katie? Do you?

(She lets go of KATIE, whose face crumples. MARY looks at KATIE for a moment. She leaves.)

Scene Three

(KATIE smiles brightly at the audience.)

KATIE: OK. So once I realised I was Jesus Christ, I knew that I had to do something. And so I went into my father's now-defunct carpentry shed, which is where I go to think these days, and suddenly it came to me. Like a vision from God, you might say, or a thunderbolt or something equally religious. And suddenly I knew what I was meant to do and so I took down some nails and some wire and some wood and for ten days and ten nights I shut myself away from the world and I worked.

On the tenth day, I emerge from the shed and I am stronger now, and I call my best friend Yasmin and she comes over to my house and I take her into the shed and I show her my work and she says "you have built a cross."

But, believe me, when I say that this isn't just a cross. It is more than seven feet tall and three feet wide and made of my father's best oak which he used to use to restore dining room tables and when I put the cross over my shoulder, I can hardly lift it but still I refuse Yasmin's help.

Yasmin and I make our way out of my father's shed with the cross and we begin to walk slowly down the street. I let Yasmin hold the bottom of my cross, which is wobbling precariously on my shoulder, but as we reach the high street I shake her off and so this is how I end up processing victoriously down the high street with my new cross, crying "there is too much suffering in the world," as I make my way passed the amazed faces of Saturday shoppers and Yasmin slowly follows me behind.

When I reach the shopping centre, I am just stopping to adjust my cross when Yasmin sees my mother coming out of the pharmacists. "Let's go," Yasmin says to me urgently. "Why?" I say, "my mother knows I'm Jesus Christ, you know." "Please."

And so we make our way slowly back to the shed and, when Yasmin is gone, I decide to find another way to show my mother I am really Jesus Christ.

(MARY enters.)

MARY: When I arrive home from the supermarket, I can't find Katie anywhere but I see the door is open in her father's shed and so I make my way slowly out there to call her in for dinner. When I come into the shed at first, I can't make out Katie, it is so dark. And then, after a moment, my eyes begin to focus and I see her. She has suspended herself somehow upon a huge seven foot wooden cross and is hanging on the cross in the darkness.

And when I see her, at first, I cannot believe my eyes, I think it must be a mistake, it can't be my daughter there suspended from a cross, but then she looks at me and she says "Mum."

And she smiles as if to say, "look what I have done. I have built a cross, I really am Jesus Christ, if I died for man's sins, maybe this will make everything alright."

And so, very slowly, I feel myself make my way through the darkness towards the cross and when I get there Katie says "no" but I already have my hands on the first hook and I am reaching up releasing her arm from the cross and as she begins to thrash at me, to pull away, to cry "I am Jesus Christ, leave me alone to die," I lean over and I say to her, "you are *not* Jesus Christ and you are never going to bring your father back. You are just a girl. You are just my daughter. And I am your mother. And I love you. And I am going to save you." and I take Katie down and I carry her, weeping and shaking in my arms, and I put her to bed. Because that is all you can do, isn't it?

You want to believe there is a God worth believing in, but in the end all you can do is put your children to bed and tuck in the sheets and turn off the lights and tell them, promise them, that everything will be alright.

Sometimes I think heaven must be a place filled with a million mothers tucking their children into bed and making sure that they are alright.

END OF PLAY

WHEN IT RAINS
Lauren Feldman

CHARACTERS & SETTING

SOUP *(Mara), age twenty-one*
LYNN, *age forty-five*

Time: mid to late September, 2005

Place: SOUP'*s apartment, New England*

(Mid to late Spetember, the living room of SOUP'*s apartment.* SOUP *and* LYNN *are onstage. Neither is looking at the other.* LYNN *is drenched.)*

(A beat, then SOUP *talks to us.)*

SOUP: Two summers before my mom ran away, I was eleven, sixth grade, we went on a family vacation. To the Grand Canyon. I have virtually no recollection of what the Grand Canyon actually looks like, or what it was like standing inside of it, or the oranges and reds I see it having in all those publicity shots. Which kind of makes me think that no matter what good things you do for your kids before age, like, twenty, they're not going to remember it anyway. So why dish out the dough for a family vacation to the fucking Grand Canyon?

Maybe that's not entirely true. But here's what I do remember. I remember my mom, Dad, and I decided to hike down into the North Rim or South Rim or Pacific Rim or something, and I'm begging Dad to let us hike all the way down to the canyon floor, because how cool would that be? And Dad looks at my mom and I see that look that means "Honey, no." And my mother says to me "We'll see." Yeah. Right.

So we keep hiking down, and it's hot, I think, and dusty, probably, and fun—an adventure—I do remember that. And we get, like, a third down into the canyon—we've only been walking, like, half-an-hour—and my mom says "That's far enough." And I'm arguing that it's only another, like, forty-five minutes to the canyon floor. And there's a river there and a campsite and a canteen with water and greenery, and you can't come all the way to the GRAND CANYON without going all the way down to the canyon floor. It's like sucking a Blow-Pop and then THROWING AWAY THE GUM. But Mom says, "It takes three times longer to climb back up—that's plenty climbing for all of us." Yeah, "We'll see," my butt.

So we drink from our canteens from, like, Walmart that Mom bought us, and we start back up. Mom's right—it is harder. But it's pleasant. I feel my legs pulling, pushing, and I'm becoming a warrior. And there's a breeze I think, or maybe it's just our shoes that keep kicking up the dust, and it's like a scene out of Indiana Jones. After about five minutes, Mom stops. She says she has to rest. Dad looks at her. I look at her. She says she's sorry. "No problem," I say.

We start again. Like, five more minutes and she stops again. She leans against the canyon wall, and takes deep breaths, and drinks from her canteen. "What's wrong?" My voice sounds high-pitched. "Nothing, sweetie. I just need to catch my breath." But I don't see her panting, or turning blue in the face or anything. She just holds her shirt over her nose and mouth and keeps breathing. I've seen her do this before, when we're passing a construction site or something. But now she's leaning against the canyon wall, and it looks like it's holding her up. Her limbs are just hanging from her body. Her eyes are big. She's taking deep breaths with lots of concentration.

And suddenly I think: this isn't allergies. This is my mother.

I look at Dad and he's not looking at me; he's looking at Mom and saying "Why don't we send Soup up and she can get help?" And Mom says, muffled, "She can't go by herself." And Dad says, "Then I'll go." "I'm fine," Mom says and stands—because if there's one thing I do know about her, it's that she'd never fracture a family.

We're not allowed to take separate flights—if the airplane crashes, she wants us all to be on it.

And now a couple's approaching—an older woman and her grown son. They ask are we okay, do we need any help, or water? Dad smiles, makes a joke, says we're fine, and he thanks them. They pass in front of us and I see the older woman, with her backpack and her walking stick, hiking easily ahead of her son. I look at Dad, who's looking at the canyon. I look at Mom, who's looking there too. So I say "Whatever, Mom. However long it takes." And she nods that nod that means, "If I open my mouth, I'm going to cry."

We keep going, moving very slowly, and we coach her. "Come on, Mom, you can do it. Good job, Mom. You're doing great. Keep it up, you're almost there."

And then—finally—we make it. We crest out on top, and as I move away from the edge of the canyon, I feel my legs releasing. In my chest, it feels like a fist is opening. I exhale. Long.

Anyway, that's what I remember of the Grand Canyon.

Two summers later, my mother runs away. She marries a man in New England, divorces my dad in Miami, and everything—

I was going to say goes to hell. Whatever. Changes.

(LYNN *changes position.* SOUP *changes position.* LYNN *talks to us.*)

LYNN: There was this one time, it must have been four years ago, I looked up my daughter on the web. My daughter Soup. Because it had been quite some time since we'd talked and I wanted to know what she was up to, who she was becoming. She was listed on her high school's website as having been nominated for an award for service in a particular area—and her area was early childhood and family studies. My first thought was, well I've certainly given her enough fodder... But my second thought was, my goodness, Soup—you take after me.

I clicked on that square in the top right corner, the one that makes things bigger or smaller, and— oh wait a minute. Or is that the one that doesn't work for pictures? Maybe I just double-clicked on the photo? I don't remember. I'm sure you know. Toby keeps trying to show me. I think it's just one of those things I'm born without an affinity for. Like Florida.

Anyhow, I somehow manage, by some miracle of God, to make this photo bigger, and I just sit there looking at my daughter as a young woman now. Her face has cleared up—the texture of her skin has changed. Her whole face looks fuller—rounded cheeks, a broad forehead. She must have curves now, breasts, full breasts, and I wager whether she takes after my side of the family (C-cup) or Steve's (A-cup). Not that Steve wore a bra. And she's wearing lipstick. And eyeliner. And all I can think of is the time she came into the bathroom and I had just sprayed my hair—she took one whiff, clapped her hands over her nose and mouth, and fell to the floor gagging.

I look at her forehead and, though I wish it weren't still there, thank God it is—the cleft. The cleft between her eyebrows that grooved itself in at age ten and never went away.

And then I notice her shirt. *(Beat)* It's my shirt. From college.

And then I get booted off-of-line because Toby logs on from the study upstairs. Now we have something that's wireless, so... No one gets booted any more.

Toby came home yesterday, from teaching, he teaches linguistics at the college here. He's also a gifted bassoonist. He comes home, he says "Lynnie." "Yes?" "The strangest thing." "What's that," I ask, absorbed in my lesson plan for, of all things, *The Runaway Bunny*. "I have two new students in my class." "Oh?" "They just came today. Oscar's finally opening up the place to the displaced kids—of Tulane, U N O, ..." "Well that's lovely," I say, "what a lovely gesture." "Soup's in my class."

(Beat)

*(*SOUP *hands* LYNN *a towel.)*

(To SOUP*)* Beautiful place. Thank you.

SOUP: It's okay. I think it came out okay.

LYNN: It came out great. I like that.

SOUP: Oh, thanks. From a friend.

LYNN: It looks great.

SOUP: An ex, actually.

LYNN: Oh.

(Beat)

SOUP: Do you want to sit?

LYNN: Sure. *(She goes to the chair.)* I'm sorry—I'm dripping.

SOUP: No, it's fine.

LYNN: Cool chairs.

(The chairs are pretty nondescript.)

SOUP: Thanks.

*(*LYNN *covers the chair with the towel and sits on that.)*

SOUP: You're soaking.

LYNN: I'm sorry.

SOUP: No, it's fine.

LYNN: It's torrential out there.

SOUP: I'm sorry you came all this way in it.

LYNN: No...

SOUP: We could have rescheduled it.

LYNN: I was already on my way.

SOUP: Are you hungry?

LYNN: No, I'm fine. I tried to call you—the service must be down.

SOUP: Yeah, it's been crazy rain like this all week.

LYNN: The roads were flooded....

SOUP: You should have just turned around.

LYNN: I'm not sure I could've. Are *you* hungry? You must be famished.

SOUP: Not really. Are you cold?

LYNN: I'm fine.

SOUP: I'm sorry the parking lot's so far.

LYNN: Nah, it's my own fault for forgetting my umbrella.

SOUP: I know—I thought that was, like, a staple.

LYNN: I'm getting old, what can I tell ya?

SOUP: Doesn't look like it.

LYNN: Well you'll just have to trust me. *(Beat)* I really love your place.

SOUP: Thanks.

LYNN: I didn't realize you were at Tulane.

SOUP: I wasn't. I was at U N O.

LYNN: Oh, how was it?

SOUP: I'm not sure; it was hit by a hurricane before I could form an opinion.

LYNN: I'm sorry. Of course. How long were you there?

SOUP: Like, a week.

LYNN: A week?

SOUP: Yeah. I'd just moved in.

LYNN: But... so, where have you been going to school?

SOUP: I haven't. I've been working. *(Beat.)*

LYNN: Oh. *(Beat)* So you're a freshman.

SOUP: Yes.

LYNN: Oh, I didn't know. Well how was that, working?

SOUP: Fine.

LYNN: Where did you work?

SOUP: Around.

LYNN: Anywhere specifically?

SOUP: No.

LYNN: What did you do?

SOUP: A lot.

LYNN: Well, how do you like it here, then? What do you think of— [the Northeast]?

SOUP: I don't know, Lynn, I just got here. *(To us, or herself)* Fuck.

LYNN: *(To us, or herself)* Fuck.

(Beat)

SOUP: I'm gonna go make some tea.

LYNN: I can do it.

SOUP: That's all right.

LYNN: No, I'd like to.

SOUP: It's fine.

LYNN: Mara, it's fine.

(LYNN exits. Beat)

SOUP: This is silly. It's my house. Or apartment, whatever.

LYNN: *(O S)* I've already started.

SOUP: Then stop.

(LYNN appears. SOUP exits. LYNN talks to us.)

LYNN: I read once, in a poem, that all our ages stay with us. That when you turn another age, you're not leaving the other ages behind; you bring them with you. Whether you want to or not. So when you're twenty-one [as Soup is], you're also sixteen and fourteen and two. And when you're forty-five [as I am], you're eleven, and you're twenty-one, and you're thirty-four, and you're thirteen. Sometimes, if I think about it like that, things can start to make sense. *(She looks out the window at the rain. To* SOUP*)* It's really coming down.

SOUP: *(O S)* Sounds like it.

LYNN: It's like it was in Miami.

SOUP: *(Entering with a tea tray)* Yeah, except in Miami, it stops.

LYNN: How is Miami?

SOUP: It's still there.

LYNN: Good....

SOUP: [It's] Fine. Hot.

LYNN: How's your father?

(SOUP looks at her.)

SOUP: He's okay.

LYNN: Is he?

SOUP: Well he collapsed last year and no one knew why, and then they did an E K G and found he'd had a

heart attack. He's fine now. They have him on meds—
Lipitor—and he's watching his cholesterol. In case
you've forgotten, heart disease runs in his family,
and Grandpa died at fifty. Dad just turned fifty-four.
(To us) But I don't know what saying that accomplishes,
so I say: *(To* LYNN*)* He's good.

LYNN: Good.

SOUP: He's not seeing anyone. How's Toby?

LYNN: He's good, thanks.

(Beat)

(The tea kettle whistles—thank God. LYNN *starts,
but* SOUP *exits instead.* LYNN *looks around the apartment.*
LYNN *breathes.)*

SOUP: *(O S)* Milk?

LYNN: No, thank you.

*(*SOUP *enters with the pot of tea.)*

LYNN: My goodness, what service.

*(*SOUP *fills the mugs.)*

LYNN: Honey?

*(*SOUP *looks at her.)*

LYNN: Do you have honey?

SOUP: No. Sorry. I thought you were allergic...

LYNN: I used to be.

SOUP: Not any more?

LYNN: Apparently not.

(They fill the beat with tea.)

SOUP: Dad's thinking of selling the house.

LYNN: Is he? Why?

SOUP: Retirement. Move somewhere else. He liked
Arizona.

LYNN: I remember.

SOUP: You guys talk about retirement?

LYNN: Your father and I?

SOUP: Toby and you.

LYNN: Oh. Sometimes. We're still a ways off. But we
like it here.

SOUP: I'm sure.

LYNN: Did he ask your opinion?

SOUP: Toby?

LYNN: Your father.

SOUP: Yeah.

LYNN: What did you say?

SOUP: Honestly? I said if this is what the South
is coming to, if we're gonna be onslaughted with
hurricanes from A to Z, REPEATEDLY, every season
from now on in this new, what, twenty-year cycle of
hurricane activity, I say sell the house. Because it's only
a matter of time before it's our house that's decimated.
I don't think there's any way that anyone in Miami
will be left standing at the end of twenty years. *(To us)*
But what I actually say is: *(To* LYNN*)* Whatever. I told
him I don't care.

LYNN: We talk about retirement all the time. I'd like to
teach Adult Literacy. I want to write children's books.
Toby wants to stay in New England for part of the year
and then travel together during the winters. He talks
about learning new languages—Dutch, Swahili—eating
exotic foods. I want to see Africa. In all my life, I never
thought I'd say that, but here I am and I'm saying it, I

want to see Africa. *(To us)* But what I say is: *(To* SOUP*)*
Mango?

SOUP: Mango Ceylon with Vanilla.

LYNN: Mm. I should see if they carry it by me.

SOUP: A friend recommended it.

LYNN: An ex?

SOUP: No.

LYNN: Are you seeing anyone?

SOUP: No.

LYNN: Making friends?

SOUP: Sure.

LYNN: Are people friendly here?

SOUP: Of course.

LYNN: Are... Are you still on meds?

SOUP: That's none of your business. *(To us)* But I say:
(To LYNN*)* No.

LYNN: Was that what your doctor advised?

*(*SOUP *"spills" her tea.)*

SOUP: Oops.

LYNN: Oh, careful. Are you okay?

SOUP: I'm fine.

LYNN: Here.

*(*SOUP *starts for the kitchen.)*

LYNN: No you stay there.

*(*SOUP *stops and lets* LYNN *exit.)*

SOUP: It's just a wet sort of day.

*(*LYNN *reenters with paper towels. Lots. She starts to clean.)*

SOUP: I can do it.

LYNN: I got it.

SOUP: Here...

LYNN: Don't worry. It's nothing. *(She is cleaning the table.)* See? *(She is cleaning the floor.)* It's all done.

(LYNN exits. SOUP dries her clothes. LYNN reenters with a wet paper towel, and wipes down the table and floor.)

LYNN: Easy.

(LYNN exits to throw away the trash. SOUP waits. SOUP looks at us—a silent plea for help?)

LYNN: *(O S)* Mara, where's your garbage can?

(SOUP starts to answer.)

LYNN: *(O S)* No, wait, I found it. Oh. That's not it. Where is it, Mar?

SOUP: *(To us, or herself)* My name is Soup.

LYNN: *(O S)* Mar?

SOUP: Across from the sink.

LYNN: *(O S)* Where?

SOUP: Just directly across from the sink.

LYNN: *(O S)* I don't see it.

SOUP: It's literally exactly across from where the sink is. *(Pause)* Underneath the cabinet...

(The sound of cabinets opening and closing.)

SOUP: Directly across from the sink...

(LYNN laughs. SOUP doesn't.)

SOUP: Just leave it on the counter and I'll throw it away later.

LYNN: *(O S)* This is a riot... *(She reenters, still holding the paper towels.)*

SOUP: Here.

(SOUP brings the living room wastebasket to LYNN.)

LYNN: It's got food on it.

SOUP: It's just tea.

LYNN: Won't you get ants?

(Pause. SOUP exits with the paper towels to the kitchen.)

LYNN: Or maybe you don't get ants around here....

SOUP: *(O S)* Oh. *(She reenters.)* I moved it behind the pantry.

LYNN: Well good, because I didn't think I was senile *yet*. So you don't think you'd get ants?

SOUP: *(To us)* Oh my God please give me strength. *(Beat)* I think, of all my deep dark fears—and I have many—I think the scariest is that, despite all best efforts, I am going to become my mother. Without even realizing it. I do this— *(Her hand makes a small gesture/mannerism—such as circling the fingertips of her thumb and pointer finger around each other.)* —all the time. I do this, and I watched my mother doing this the whole time I was growing up, and I remember thinking, Who does this?

(LYNN exits to the bedroom.)

SOUP: And then she left and one day I caught my hand doing this without my permission. So I made a conscious decision that of everything I would NOT emulate, THIS topped the list. And THIS is the thing I catch myself doing ALL THE TIME. Why is that?! Why does something like this— *(She does it.)* —have to be genetic? Why waste a gene on— [this?] *(She does it again.)* It drives me bonkers. Because it feels so

NATURAL. And if I can't even control— [this] *(She does it again.)* —then I don't even stand a chance at changing the bigger things. Which makes me dreadfully fuckfully afraid that I am going to become my mother.

*(*LYNN *enters wearing* SOUP's *clothes—boxers, socks, t-shirt?)*

LYNN: I hope you don't mind. I was cold.

SOUP: Oh. Why didn't you say something?

*(*LYNN *shrugs.)*

SOUP: Do you wanna take a hot shower?

LYNN: No, this is good. Dry clothes.

SOUP: I have other things.

LYNN: These are fine. I love the socks. What?

SOUP: You look young.

LYNN: Well my goodness, I should wear this more often. Trick people—

SOUP: Young-ER.

LYNN: —into believing that I'm only forty-five.

SOUP: Is that how old you are?

LYNN: The last time I checked.

SOUP: And how long ago was that?

(They almost smile.)

SOUP: What happened?

LYNN: What?

*(*SOUP *indicates a bruise on Mom's knee.)*

LYNN: Oh...I bumped into one of the kids' desks.

SOUP: Ouch.

LYNN: Yeah. It didn't hurt at the time.

(Beat)

SOUP: Is that the truth?

LYNN: Is what the truth?

SOUP: The kid's desk.

(Beat)

LYNN: It was probably the truth. Honestly I can't remember.

SOUP: It's not... Toby [is it?]

LYNN: How dare you. How the fuck dare you. *(To us)* But I say: *(To SOUP)* No. God no. No, Soup, I wish you knew him.

SOUP: Yeah. There are a lot of things I wish. *(To us)* And suddenly I'm not sure if I actually said that out loud.

(What to say now? What not to say?)

LYNN: Did you get my letters?

SOUP: Yeah. *(Beat)* You want more tea?

LYNN: Um, sure.

(SOUP pours.)

LYNN: It must have been a hell of an experience. *(Clarifying)* Katrina.

SOUP: I wouldn't know; we were evacuated.

LYNN: I'm glad you were. I can't imagine —

SOUP: There were babies that drowned. I *was* one. I— Whoa. That's so not what I meant to say. I meant to say I *saw* one. Bobbing. I saw one bobbing. A baby. On T V. I saw dogs and cats stranded on roofs and tree limbs, howling for their owners. I saw hotlines for lost children and photos on websites. There's a boy— Matthew Allen—blond, skinny, ten years old—I still don't think they've found him. Disappeared clean off

the face of the earth, like the winds just blew him away.
There are kids in these centers—all these one inch by
one inch boxes of children—square photos—in long
columns and rows—dozens and dozens of children's
pictures—children looking for parents—parents
looking for children—and the saddest are the children
looking for parents because they're sitting in these
centers, abandoned and lost and completely powerless
to find these parents WHO I DON'T THINK ARE
EVEN LOOKING FOR THEM. *(To us)* But all that
fucking comes out is: *(To* LYNN*)* I can't believe it's
still raining.

LYNN: *(To us)* I watch the news. Pretty religiously.
I can't seem to tear my eyes from it. I see all these
children—in the Gulf, in Thailand, Pakistan, Cuba,
Indonesia, in godforsaken Darfur, in fucking Iraq. I see
these children and I look for the spark. I look hard into
their eyes. And at their chapped and bleeding lips for
any sign of joy. Or childhood. I think it's been
kidnapped. I think you all have been— [kidnapped.]

SOUP: Is that your phone?

*(*LYNN*'s cell phone has been ringing.)*

LYNN: Oh. *(She locates the phone and checks the caller.
A moment as she decides how to handle this. Then: into
phone)* Hello? ...Hi sweetie.... Actually, I'm visiting
Soup.... Soup. Your sister.... Yes you do. You remember
I told you the story of the little girl who traveled in
a pouch at my chest? Like a marsupial? Mara the
marsoup— ...I don't know when.... Listen, can you tell
Daddy I'll call him back later? ...I miss you too, baby....
Bye bye.

*(*LYNN *hangs up. Beat)*

SOUP: Two, right? Children?

LYNN: Well, three.

SOUP: Two.

LYNN: *(To us)* And suddenly I'm not sure if I heard that out loud or in my head.

SOUP: Congratulations. Gotta pee.

(SOUP exits. LYNN talks to us.)

LYNN: Three years after she was born, she developed the habit of throwing fits. I teach second grade, I work with children all the time, so I know that fits can be common behavior. But they're not *appropriate* behavior, and Steve and I decided they were something that would need to stop. And when I say fits, I mean tempests. I mean full-force tantrums, of screaming and kicking and howling, pounding her fists on the floor—she'd scream until she started coughing, she'd cough until she started choking, she'd choke until she went hoarse, and eventually she'd fall asleep. And so we had to teach her, this is not an appropriate expression of emotion, that there are other, more communicative ways of emoting. Eventually the tantrums died away, except every now and again one would rear its awful head, and there was nothing anyone could do about it but run for cover.

Well this one day, she was on the floor as usual, tears and arms and legs flying, her little face beet-red, and I just looked at her and thought:

"Who are you? Who are you, little girl? Where did you come from? Because you did not come from me, or my mother—we don't do that. You did not come from Steve, or his parents, they don't do that. Who are you?"

And I thought of leaving. I thought, I don't need this. This isn't what it is to be a mother. This isn't my child. She's a changeling. She's possessed. Something is seriously wrong with this girl's wiring. If I don't leave, THIS is what I'll be stuck with for the rest of my life.

I don't know if any of you have ever witnessed a childhood tantrum. If you haven't, let me just tell you,

after the first fifty or so times, you swear you're going
to kill yourself.

Sometimes I think it's amazing I didn't.

But on this one particular day, with her father at work
and Soup on the floor, choking on her lung—and at the
time I thought I was pregnant again—on this one day I
left Soup screaming on the floor, and I brought the pad
of post-its and a pen over to the couch, and I made a
list of pros and cons, one thought per post-it. And after
about ten minutes, when I'd pretty much run out of
things to weigh, I grouped the post-its on my left for
pros and on my right for cons, and I had one more con
than I had pros. And I thought...

Well, it surprised me. I never would have thought
myself someone who would have one more con against
being a mother. I raised my brother. In a way I raised
my mother. I just never would have thought.

I walked over to the phone and I dialed Steve at work,
and I waited for him to answer so I could say, "Tell me
to stay." I waited. I waited until the phone disconnected
me.

So I walked back to the post-it piles, Soup starting to
go hoarse now with coughing, and I picked up the cons,
and I took the top two, and I ate them. I did. I actually
crumpled and swallowed them. And I looked at the
piles, and now there was one more pro than con,
so I stayed.

And when Soup fell asleep, I put her to bed.

And when Steve came back home, I smiled and said
"Good night," and I walked into our bedroom and
closed the door.
(*She looks toward the exit.*) She's always been a lingerer.
She's a quick thinker, but she's always been a little slow
in the Life Department.

(SOUP *reenters with a plate of cookies and prepares a new
round of tea.*)

SOUP: Want more?

LYNN: Yes. *(Silence. To us)* She was probably in fifth grade when she was in the tail-end of one of her tantrums. She was upset over, honestly, I don't remember what—and it was a Saturday, because Steve was there—and she yelled at us and Steve said something back—and she stormed to the front door, flung it open, and hollered, "Leave me alone. I'm running away."
And I said, "Where are you going to go?"
And she said, "Anywhere but here."
And Steve said, "Great. We'll help you pack."
And this look crossed her face. *(Beat)* And I could see it—this moment of this child, my daughter, weighing the post-its. I wanted her to be thirty-four, so she could understand that these moments happen, so I could tell her "I felt the same thing," so I could say "There will be more post-its for you to leave, but you have to eat two of them," I wanted her to be able to understand the complexity of love and the ties that bind a family— how knotted and webby and frayed and moldy they can get, but how they're actually inescapable.
I saw the tears well up... and she stormed into her room, slammed the shit out of the door, and silence. I looked at Steve—it was one of the moments of—another of those moments of "Who are you?" He looked me in the eyes and walked away. So I closed the front door. And then I locked it.
I sometimes wonder whether a piece of you leaves bit by bit because of certain things. Said, or done, or happened to you. Whether that sears off a part of your spirit or something, so we become less and less...whole.

(SOUP breaks off a piece of a cookie and eats it.)

SOUP: Dig in if you want.

LYNN: I'm okay.

SOUP: I know it's not gourmet or anything.

LYNN: No, we have these all the time at home. *(Beat)* I should probably go pretty soon.

SOUP: Whenever.

LYNN: Homework Detail.

SOUP: Here, take 'em to go.

LYNN: No, no, that's sweet of you.

SOUP: Take some for your kids. *(Beat)*

LYNN: Thanks. I still have a few minutes.

SOUP: Whatever you need.

(Pause)

(Silence)

(LYNN looks at the rain.)

LYNN: Think it's gonna stop?

SOUP: Dunno. *(She talks to us.)* And it doesn't. Within a month, Hurricane Wilma pummels Miami—not to mention Cancun and the Keys and the D R and most of Cuba. Meanwhile the alphabet RESTARTS with Hurricane Alpha brewing up in the Atlantic. I come home one day and on my answering machine there is a message from my father:
   "Hi Soup. Listen, I'm fine and the house is fine. There's some minor roof damage and our patio blew away. There's no power and no phone, so all I have is my cell. I'll call when I can. But I'm fine. Don't worry. Love you, pup.... Bye."
   And I'm trying to picture the patio—the forty-foot-long screened-in metal structure, anchored to the ground and attached to the house—I'm trying to imagine it ripped up from the earth, torn off from the concrete, and blown away. Where does a forty-foot metal structure blow TO? Where does it land? Whose

roof does it puncture? Whose patio punctures ours?
I later learn that every house in our whole region loses
their backyards and parts of their roofs, and that the
masts of trees and of the thickest power poles snap
and collapse in the roads, so driving becomes an
obstacle course—a flooded one—without streetlamps
or stoplights. I later learn that the patio is the least of
the damage—that the not-so-major roof stuff is actually
major indeed and the house floods and our belongings
rot and there's no power and it takes ages just to
ascertain what to do with the house and how to rebuild
it. I later learn that Dad is in the hospital for all of this,
for all of the storm, in fact, and that the hospital loses
air conditioning, running water, and flushing toilets,
that it prohibits all visitors, and basically functions for
48 hours in a state of lock-down. I learn that Dad is in
the hospital because of chest pains and that leads to a
double bypass and then they keep him in the hospital
because he's retaining fluid in his lungs and because
he's been coughing so much that he's loosened the wire
holding his ribcage together. They talk about going
back in to tighten it. I learn they've got him on two
diuretics simultaneously. So he can pee out the fluid in
his lungs - quickly. I guess so that he doesn't drown.

All this I will learn. In my little one-bedroom
apartment in a foreign city in the upper half of the
country. And when I look down.... (*She sees that her
fingers are doing the gesture.*)

LYNN: Can I read you something? It'll only take a
minute.

SOUP: (*Stuck*) Sure.

(LYNN *goes to get her book.*)

SOUP: I don't remember it, but Dad says she read to me
all while growing up. She probably read to me in utero.
When she and Dad were newly married and happy,
and her voice absorbed into his sperm and her eggs so

they were suffused with it when I was conceived.
And then I was born drunk with words. Fetal Literacy
Syndrome.
   I'm sure I adored it growing up, until I hit, you know,
thirteen and was like, "Please don't read me picture
books any more."

LYNN: *When It Rains...* by Caroline Gruff. Illustrations—

SOUP: Wait—what?

LYNN: —by Marty Silverman.

SOUP: You wrote a children's book?

LYNN: To: My Soup.
"Where the wandering water gushes
From the hills above Glen-Car,
In pools among—"

SOUP: You didn't write that.

LYNN: Mister Yeats provided the epigram.

(LYNN *continues.* SOUP *moves away?*)

(*Very subtly, the lights start to change—until it's clear that
Lynn is reading directly to us.*)

LYNN: "In pools among the rushes
That scarce could bathe a star...
Come away, O human child!
To the waters and the wild
With a faery hand in hand,
For the world's more full of weeping
Than you can understand."
(*She looks up. She checks in with us.*)
When It Rains... by Caroline Gruff.
"When it rains, I go inside my house..."

(*The lights fade to black.*)

WAYS YOU CAN SURVIVE THE WORLD
PART THREE: HIBERNATE
Jennifer Tuckett

CHARACTERS & SETTING

YASMIN, *aged fourteen*
AZMA, YASMIN's *mother.*

The set should be minimal and does not need to be realistic.

Scene One

(YASMIN, *to the audience, in bed.*)

YASMIN: I am fourteen years, eleven months, twenty four days and three hours old exactly, when I come up with the perfect solution to life. Obviously this is a bit of a feat, coming up with the perfect solution to life at nearly fifteen—no fourteen—years old, but there you go. Either you've got it or you haven't right?
(She hesitates.)
I call my. I call my perfect solution to life "*no experience*". By "no experience", I mean that my plan is to forsake or forgo everything that is dangerous. I will no longer travel to new countries in case the aeroplane I am travelling in happens to be blown up or the place I am visiting turns out to be unexpectedly horrible or dangerous or both. I will no longer travel into the city in case the train or tube or bus I am travelling on becomes the victim of a terrorist attack. I will no longer walk outside in case I am unprovokedly savaged by a wild dog or accosted by a boy with a gun who tries to rob me and ends up shooting me with his gun and neither of us really know why. I will no longer talk to people on the phone because, well, frankly, this always makes me feel nervous and as if I'm not good enough and if I'm going to give up all this other stuff, I might as well take the opportunity to give up something I find really soul-destroying as well, right?
(She smiles.)
In short, I am going to hibernate.
(She smiles again.)
And when I think of this, this so simple plan, I feel

inside me this huge wave of relief that I no longer have
to face these things anymore and I go upstairs to my
room and I pull down my books from my bookcase
and I begin to plan, and when my plan is finished,
I get changed into my pyjamas and I curl up in bed
and I am so happy that I am going to stay in bed
forever. I am so happy at this thought. I really am.
(She reaches over and switches off the bedside light.)

Scene Two

*(YASMIN, in bed. She is sleeping in semi-darkness. A long
moment passes. AZMA enters the bedroom in work clothes.
She sits down on the end of YASMIN's bed, watching her
sleep. Another long moment passes. Suddenly, YASMIN sits
up and switches on the light.)*

YASMIN: What are you doing, Mum?

AZMA: Yamsin—

YASMIN: I'm trying to sleep.

AZMA: Yasmin, I—

YASMIN: I'm trying to hibernate—

AZMA: Yasmin, I—

YASMIN: What the fuck are you doing in my hibernation
cell?

AZMA: I just wanted to watch you sleep.

*(YASMIN grabs her glasses. She puts them on and pushes
them up her nose.)*

YASMIN: Please.

AZMA: What?

YASMIN: Do you not know that being disturbed during hibernation is one of the reasons why so many animals are becoming extinct?

AZMA: I'm sorry, I didn't know that—

YASMIN: Well, now you do. O K?
(She takes off her glasses and lies back down to sleep.)

AZMA: *(Hesitating)* Although you did say I could disturb you to bring you your food, Yasmin—

(YASMIN sighs. She sits back up.)

YASMIN: That's different, Mum.

AZMA: *(Hesitating)* I see.

YASMIN: Have you brought me my food at *(She puts on her glasses and checks her watch)* half past twelve at night? No. I don't think so. O K?

AZMA: But I—

YASMIN: WHAT?

AZMA: I just wanted to check in on you, Yasmin. That's all.

YASMIN: I see. Well, you've checked in on me. And everything is great. I'm having a terrific time hibernating. Things couldn't be better. O K?

AZMA: *(Hesitating)* No.

(YASMIN sighs. She takes her glasses off. She polishes them. She pushes them up her nose again.)

AZMA: You can't stay in bed forever, Yasmin.

YASMIN: Why not?

AZMA: Because you're not...a bear.

YASMIN: *(Confused)* A bear?

AZMA: You can't hibernate.

YASMIN: Look, Mum, actually bears don't hibernate.

(AZMA *looks at* YASMIN.)

YASMIN: They don't.

(AZMA *looks at* YASMIN.)

YASMIN: Really. Whilst the bear's heart rate is slow, the bear's body temperature remains relatively stable and it can be easily roused.

(AZMA *looks at* YASMIN.)

YASMIN: Therefore it is merely in a state of torpor rather than hibernation.

(AZMA *looks at* YASMIN.)

YASMIN: For god's sake. What have I done now?

(*A long pause*)

AZMA: Where is this coming from, Yasmin?

(YASMIN *sighs. She ducks back under the covers. After a moment, she emerges with a book.*)

YASMIN: (*Holding up the book*) From here.

(AZMA *stares at* YASMIN. YASMIN *sighs again and, finding the right page, opens the book.*)

YASMIN: (*Reading*) "Since 2000, there have been big steps forward in the possibility of inducing hibernation in human beings. For example, at the University of Washington, hibernation has been induced in mice by subjecting them to large doses of Hydrogen sulphide. The mice subsequently emerged from their hibernation unharmed and were able to resume their normal lives." (*She looks at her mother.*) You see?

AZMA: I'm not subjecting you to large doses of...of...whatever it's called, Yasmin.

YASMIN: I'M NOT ASKING YOU TO. *(She sighs.)* I'm sorry.

AZMA: It's fine. I'm just having difficulty processing your decision to give up on life, Yasmin. That's...all.

YASMIN: You should read the book, Mum. It's fascinating. For example, my book says that if blood is taken from a hibernating squirrel in the winter and injected into another squirrel in the spring, the spring squirrel will not be able to help but fall into hibernation. *(Beat)* Isn't that amazing? For someone to be able to decide when you need to withdraw from your life for a while?

AZMA: I'm not sure—

YASMIN: Once more research has been done, I expect hibernation will be the normal thing for human beings.

AZMA: I don't think hibernation will ever be the normal thing for human beings, Yasmin.

YASMIN: That's because you're not thinking about this in the right way, Mum! Think of all the good it could do. Injured soldiers could be put into hibernation until help can reach the battlefield. Accident victims could be saved. Astronauts could hibernate for hundreds of years. People could lose weight.

AZMA: Why does this sound like a science fiction story to me?

(YASMIN frowns.)

YASMIN: I don't know. Because you're being stupid? *(She sighs.)* Hibernation...*is* normal, Mum. It's *us* who aren't normal. Putting ourselves through all this. Getting on trains. Going into work. Driving cars. Blowing each other up. That's not normal, Mum.

(AZMA looks at YASMIN.)

YASMIN: Hibernation is all about preserving yourself.

(AZMA *looks at* YASMIN.)

YASMIN: It is.

(Beat)

AZMA: Yasmin. *(She hesitates.)* Yasmin. *(She hesitates.)* Yasmin...where is this coming from? *(She hesitates.)* And why...do you...my little fifteen—

YASMIN: *(Frowning)* I'm fourteen, I'm still fourteen!

AZMA: —fourteen year old girl, need to hibernate?

(YASMIN *is silent.*)

AZMA: What have I done so wrong?

(YASMIN *is silent.*)

AZMA: *(Hesitantly)* Have I...been such a bad mother?

(YASMIN *is silent.*)

AZMA: Have I?

(YASMIN *is silent. She looks away.*)

AZMA: Yasmin, I—

(She stops. She can't go on. YASMIN *looks at her mother fiercely.)*

YASMIN: What? Why shouldn't I hibernate? Mum?

(AZMA *is silent.*)

YASMIN: Well?

(AZMA *is silent.*)

YASMIN: Well?

(AZMA *is silent.*)

YASMIN: WELL?

(AZMA *is silent.* YASMIN *sighs loudly.*)

YASMIN: Exactly. You can't think of anything, can you, Mum? You never can.

(Y ASMIN *takes off her glasses. She lies back down.
She lies with her back to her mother.*)

(A ZMA *looks at* Y ASMIN. *She hesitates. She can't say
anything. She wants to, but she can't. She looks away.
She leaves.*)

(Y ASMIN *sits up. She watches her mother leave.
For a moment, her face falls. Just for a moment.
She lies back down and pulls the sheets over her head.*)

(*Lights fade.*)

Scene Three

(Y ASMIN, *in bed, to the audience*)

Y ASMIN: It's great here in bed. For the first two days, I
sleep almost constantly, curled up into a little ball,
the sheets pulled over my head, the world blocked out.
At the end of two days, I am temporarily and rudely
roused from my hibernation by mother as happened
in the previous scene (this happens in hibernation,
I promise, human beings are masters at disturbing
animals from their hibernation with their cars and
tractors and bombs) and, anyway, it is at this moment
that my eyes fall on my teddy bear. My teddy bear is
sitting, in an admittedly slightly dusty state (for which
I hold only myself responsible) on my bookcase and so
I get up and pull him down from the bookcase and take
him into hibernation with me.

And together we begin to create a special world.

For the first time, in nearly nine years, my teddy bear
regains his voice and begins to tell me stories like when
I was younger. Of his family. Of his childhood. Of how
everything will be alright. And under the sheet
becomes a tent, a spaceship, an adventure to the moon.

And then, after a while, after we have regained each
other's trust and have re-established a mutually

satisfying rapport, Teddy turns to me and he asks me,
his button eyes glistening with bewilderment and
innocence, why he is here, explaining that he had
thought he had retired and had lately been planning
a vacation with the other toys to Hawaii whilst lying
neglected on my bookcase.

   And so I explain to him about the plan which I call
"no experience" and human hibernation and how
it really has been developed and will be used soon
and how wonderful our new life of no experience will
be and Teddy listens to me quietly and seriously and
when I am finished he is silent for a moment, thinking,
and then he looks at me finally and says "but that
sounds like no fun, why don't we go into the city and
get drunk instead, Yasmin?"
(She pauses.)
For a moment, I am motionless, looking at my teddy
hear, as he smiles back at me innocently, all black
button eyes and sewn on smile, and then, very gently,
I pick him up in my arms, and I feel him squirm
happily, imagining that a hug is approaching and
that I will soon be burying my face in his soft but worn
plush brown fur and muttering sweet nothings about
what a clever teddy bear he is, just like I did when I was
younger and, anyway, I hold him for a moment like this
in mid-air, looking at him for the last time and then, in
one swift move, I lift him above my head and I throw
him out of the bed and he bounces for a moment on the
carpet and I see his black button eyes look at me with
terror and then he rolls under the bookcase and out
of sight and that is the last time I see his sewn on
treacherous smile *(She smiles at the audience. She pulls
the sheets back over her head. She disappears from sight.)*

Scene Four

(YASMIN *is sleeping in the semi-darkness. A long moment passes.* AZMA *enters. She sits down on the bed in the dark. Another long moment passes. Suddenly,* YASMIN *sits and switches on the light.*)

YASMIN: For fuck's sake, Mum.

AZMA: I've been thinking, Yasmin—

YASMIN: Haven't we done this already?

AZMA: Yes, Yasmin. We have but—

YASMIN: Exactly. Why do you always have to be such so fucking stupid, Mum?

(AZMA *stares at* YASMIN. YASMIN *looks back at her uncertainly. A long moment passes. Suddenly* AZMA *reaches over. She grabs* YASMIN's *wrists and begins to drag her out of bed.*)

YASMIN: What are you—

(AZMA *ignores her.*)

YASMIN: Get off—

(AZMA *ignores her.*)

YASMIN: Leave me alone—

(AZMA *ignores her.*)

YASMIN: You're hurting me—

(AZMA *ignores her.*)

YASMIN: Mummy—

(AZMA *ignores her.*)

YASMIN: Please—

(AZMA *pulls* YASMIN *out of bed. She lets go of* YASMIN's *wrists.* YASMIN *falls to the floor.* AZMA *looks at* YASMIN. *She starts to cry, to hit herself in the head repeatedly?* YASMIN *looks at her, alarmed. For a moment, it looks as if she will get up and go to* AZMA *but she is paralysed with the shock of being thrown out of her hibernation.)*

(*Instead, she claps her hands over her eyes.*)

(AZMA *looks up at* YASMIN. *She frowns.*)

AZMA: What are you doing?

YASMIN: I'm concentrating. If I concentrate really hard, I think I can get my hibernation back.

AZMA: (*Aggressively*) Fuck that.

(YASMIN *lets her hands fall. She looks at* AZMA, *surprised.*)

AZMA: What? Did you think you were the only person who knows how to swear, Yasmin? (*Beat*) Who knows how to be scared? (*Beat*) Who knows the desire to cut themselves off from the world and to hibernate? (*Beat*) Did you really think that, Yasmin? Did you? (*She begins to laugh.*)

YASMIN: You're behaving like a lunatic, Mum.

AZMA: Am I, Yasmin? Am I? Really? (*She hesitates.*) And did you think that you were the only one who was allowed to behave as a lunatic, as well?

YASMIN: (*Hesitating*) Yes? (*Beat*) So. So. I think you should calm down. And I'm. I'm going to go back to bed. And, well, we'll pretend that this never happened. Because, really, this isn't the way mothers are meant to behave and really I just think it goes to show why I need to hibernate in the first place and why you never give me any—

(YASMIN *begins to crawl back to bed.* AZMA *blocks* YASMIN.)

AZMA: I don't think we'll do that, Yasmin. *(Beat)* I don't think we'll do that, at all. *(Beat)* Because I think it is time to call this a day, isn't it? You're not a bear. You're not a squirrel. You're not a lab experiment. You're not a trauma victim. You're just my daughter.

YASMIN: But—

AZMA: No buts. You're my daughter and I am not going to let you give in in this way, Yasmin.

YASMIN: But—

AZMA: I'm not.

(Beat)

YASMIN: Why not? *(Beat)* Well? *(Beat)* Well? *(Beat)* WELL?

(Beat)

AZMA: *(Finally)* Because I won't let anything happen to you, Yasmin. I swear.

YASMIN: *(Doubtfully)* How can you not let anything happen to me? In this world?

(AZMA looks at her daughter. Beat. AZMA smiles.)

AZMA: Because I have promised you, Yasmin. That's why.

(A moment. YASMIN looks at AZMA from her position on the floor. She hesitates. AZMA smiles again. She reaches out her hand.)

Scene Five

(AZMA, to the audience)

AZMA: When the winter came when Yasmin was two years old, that long, harsh winter and a chill that penetrated me to the bones when her father left me, I crawled into a cave and I sheltered there for a while. But, although my arms were tightly pressed over my head, which was burrowing into the ground, I found that I couldn't block the world out. I couldn't block Yasmin out. And so, reluctantly, I crawled out of my cave, and despite it being winter, despite it being snowy and cold on the ground and my naked skin not being made for these conditions, I suckled Yasmin, shivering, at my naked breast. And, over the years, I have longed to take her to my breast again and to nurture her there. Because I gave up my hibernation for her.

(She pauses.)

Last year, during a particularly bleak moment, I found myself climbing the steps to the roof of Yasmin's school. And standing there, looking down at the world. And as I looked down at the world, at the images of war and terrorism and floods, I once again saw Yasmin's face. And, although she doesn't know it, it saved me. It did.

(She pauses.)

I have this dream I dream again and again recently. I am back on the roof of the school and Yasmin is standing next to me and she has come out of her hibernation and she is crying. And so I reach over. And I take her hand. And I hold it within mine. And we close our eyes. And we fly. And I show her wonderful life can be again.

(Above AZMA, *a thousand stars appear. They light up the bedroom and* YASMIN *and* AZMA. *A moment.* AZMA *and* YASMIN *look up at the stars with surprise. Then they look at each other. Maybe* YASMIN *smiles at* AZMA? *Just for a moment. Lights fade.*

END OF PLAY

www.ingramcontent.com/pod-product-compliance
Lightning Source LLC
Chambersburg PA
CBHW052158090426

42741CB00010B/2326